MANSIONS

── OF ──

MAGNATES

MANSIONS

— OF —

MAGNATES

AMERICA IN THE MAD 20TH CENTURY

LYN LINCOURT

assisted by Chris Kirk

TATE PUBLISHING
AND ENTERPRISES, LLC

Published by Tate Publishing & Enterprises, LLC
127 E. Trade Center Terrace | Mustang, Oklahoma 73064 USA
1.888.361.9473 | www.tatepublishing.com

Tate Publishing is committed to excellence in the publishing industry. The company reflects the philosophy established by the founders, based on Psalm 68:11,
"The Lord gave the word and great was the company of those who published it."

Book design copyright © 2015 by Tate Publishing, LLC. All rights reserved.
Cover design by Kristina Angela Igot
Interior design by Jimmy Sevilleno

Published in the United States of America

ISBN: 978-1-63367-479-0
Architecture / Buildings / Residential
15.03.31

CONTENTS

ACKNOWLEDGMENTS

This book was made possible by many gracious, supportive natives beginning with David and Elizabeth Creedon who sent me to St. John's High School for a copy of the history of the Xaverian Brothers in Worcester and Shrewsbury that included buying the house and land on 112 Main Street, part of Ard-na Clachan. St. John's Brother Conal approved access to the staff and use of the research material.

A history book needs enormous information and innumerable resources and people, too many to list. Most of the mansions' owners/residents and others interviewed were generous with their support and time, sharing knowledge and resources. Some were more deeply involved; i.e., Ed Flynn and Sarah Millar were interviewed for the Hobbs DVD produced at Shrewsbury's public station SPCA, with Marc Serra's expertise and patience making it possible.

Another was Pamela Boisvert at Iristhorpe who welcomed us to the 19th century Jenkins' property and history several times, including complete tours. While all were supportive, earning our gratitude, these were extraordinary. The Shrewsbury Historical Society and leading local Worcester and Shrewsbury historians, Albert B. Southwick and Michael P. Perna, Jr., have been generous in permitting use of their invaluable material on Horace Bigelow and others. The Worcester Historical Museum allowed free use of their library facilities and its contents, also granting permission to use photographs in the DVDs I produced. List of resources permitting use in publication and selected bibliography follow.

The Worcester Public Library assisted in the many hours we spent in searching records, newspaper archives, 19th and early 20th century history in books, magazines; e.g. The Worcester Magazine covering the early industrialists, and other sources were Public Domain.

The many people interviewed, including those living in the mansions, have been generous in sharing their stories. Judith McCann has been delightful in her memories of Dr. Chang and Allie Houghton. Sid Callahan and I shared Whittall history; Russell Bath, Jr. contacted me with stories about the Hobbs Estate and the Candy Mansion. Some are mentioned in the manuscript but all were hospitable. The research was often serendipitous. These five years have been a joyful experience.

My sincere thanks to everyone I met for it would not been possible without them. Lyn Lincourt and Chris Kirk, co-researchers.

DEDICATION

To my mentors, Elizabeth and David, and all the caring people who made this book possible--

HOW IT ALL BEGAN

Hearing at my first meeting with the Shrewsbury Historical Commission about the mansions built by the Worcester/Boston industrialists in Shrewsbury, which adjoins Worcester, I was enthralled as I had always admired old mansions, imagining stories of their residents. When I learned that Worcester and Shrewsbury shared the superb Lake Quinsigamond from its northern source south to Route 20 the entire length of their border, I was hooked.

I began sleuthing into the lives of the mansion residents who lived in these intriguing old estates and found their stories more fascinating than I had ever imagined.

As my research went back into nineteenth century Worcester and found the inland central city of Worcester becoming a world leader, I realized that this was the Industrial Revolution evolving and making a new society of middle- and upper-classes having and taking advantage of opportunities never possible before.

The railroads opened up the central city of Worcester with its many lakes as power sources that incited young men with their families to invent and develop mechanical gadgets, opening factories and creating great cities and countries.

It was exciting, none more so than Horace H. Bigelow, eighth generation of English emigrants, who had new ideas about shoemaking that resulted in manufacturing a pair of shoes in five minutes and bringing electricity to Worcester and Shrewsbury.

He was controversial and not welcomed by Worcester. He actually shared his profit with his workers; unheard of and bad business! When he was the leader of shoe manufacturing in Worcester and needed new challenges, he left manufacturing to become the master of entertainment for the man on the street, providing eye-popping programs for low entry prices, even free concerts. What was the man thinking? Worcester was shocked.

So he bought Shrewsbury's east shore of the lake, building an elegant mansion as fine as any in Newport where they were occupied only a few weeks in the summer season.

He built Bigelow Gardens in Worcester but White City with one thousand lights in Shrewsbury that entertained thousands for over forty years.

Another, Philip Washburn Moen, scion of the Washburn and Moen Manufacturing Company founders, built his estate, Ard-na-Clachan, on 365 acres of farmland in Shrewsbury, when the company was sold to American Steel & Wire in 1898. He built a self-supporting farm in five years that equaled any in the land, dying in 1904. It was sold to Charles H. Hutchins in 1906 who built a mansion on twelve acres between Main and Maple Avenue for his daughter in 1912, which she sold in 1926 to Henry Hovey.

In 1944, Hovey sold the mansion and fourteen acres to Worcester Foundation for Experimental Biology. The mansion became the administrative building and labs. In 1962, the third owner of the initial estate, now called the Brewer Estate, sold the remaining land to the foundation, but the mansion would house the family until 1972.

Begun by two biologists from Clark University in 1944, a third specialist in animal husbandry, Dr. Min Chueh Chang was lured from Cambridge University, England, in 1945 to live in the mansion and work in the kitchen lab. He developed "the pill," the most pervasive social change worldwide that has reduced the native population drastically in many western countries.

Chang commented that "They should use more water" when asked his view of the Pill. Some are acting like alley cats, ignoring the consequences.

Manufacturing provides jobs; electronics eliminates jobs. Manufacturers who outsourced overseas lost control of their products and are now insourcing. It seems we have to learn by erring.

But I digress, on to the Shrewsbury Mansions and their fascinating owners from industrial Worcester. Learn about the office boy who became the owner of the Worcester Telegram and, with an investigating reporter, fought Mafia control of Worcester and Providence and won.

Read about the theft of three internationally famous paintings and how they were recovered thirty years later.

Follow the story of a German boy who became a millionaire and married a 'widow' with two children, rescuing them from hardship to heirship. All these are found in stories of Shrewsbury Mansions and their occupants. So read on and enjoy!

—Lyn Lincourt and Chris Kirk,
a great co-researcher

THE MANSIONS OF SHREWSBURY

HORACE HOLLY BIGELOW
THE FOREST LAKE
QUINSIGAMOND

AT THE TURN of the twentieth century, Worcester was booming. It had begun with the change from an agricultural to an industrial world in the nineteenth century and enterprising young men had embraced the challenge to take chances and make changes.

Surprisingly, a landlocked city in central Massachusetts attracted many innovators who made Worcester an international name in the industrial world.

This is the story of several of the inventive men who made major contributions and expanded their interest to Shrewsbury where they built "summer homes" comparable to the Newport "cottages." Their mansions expressed their exuberance and none had more than Horace Holly Bigelow.

Born in Marlboro, Massachusetts, June 2, 1827, to Levi and Nancy A. Bigelow, he began pegging shoes on the farm in a shop built for the family chaise, joining with his father in hand-making shoes for the family, a common practice then. But this was an inventive youth with mechanical skills who, by age twenty in 1847 had made a contraption to cut and prepare heels for nailing, the beginning of a series of machines that simplified shoemaking by subdividing the work into teams of workers in a factory. He and his uncle Lambert Bigelow soon employed sixty men divided into departments.

In 1850, they opened a factory at 279 Pearl Street in New York City with $1000 each contributed by five local men in which they machine-made a heavy shoe named the New York brogan.

They also used prison labor in the New York House of Refuge, the first time prison labor had succeeded. For many years, he was asked to install factory systems in prisons in other parts of the country.

In 1857, he opened one in a penitentiary in Albany, New York, to make brogans for southern field hands.

He perfected his pegging machine by using a long ribbon of wood to slice pegs that were driven into the sole. This machine was set up in a prison in Troy, New York where he started a shoemaking plant in 1858. He then was in charge, for about three years, of a shoemaking plant at the prison in Providence, Rhode Island.

With the Civil War demand for army shoes, he and his brother-in-law Harvey T. Buck opened a prison factory in Trenton, New Jersey, making army shoes and hand-sewed women's shoes until 1868.

Meanwhile, in 1863, Bigelow became interested in a new business in Worcester, the Bay State Shoe Company.

He, Charles D. Bigelow, Lambert Bigelow, and others became involved. Horace Bigelow owned controlling interest, was manager and factory superintendent. Some four hundred to five hundred were employed for many years. The Company had about a thousand hands when three prison factories were included.

Bigelow always had multiple projects during his inventive shoemaking years, including financial backing of other companies such as the Bullard Repeating Arms Company in Springfield until he proposed in the late 1800s to give all its machinery to Worcester Polytechnic Institute for a training school believing that it be would both useful and self-supporting (SPY undated).

WPI Library Associate Director of Research Christine Drew confirmed this in "Seventy Years of the Worcester Polytechnic Institute" published in 1937. A summer training program in WPI shops instigated by the Mechanics Association opened in 1883 but closed in 1890 due to lack of money.

In 1891, Horace H. Bigelow offered WPI a complete set of Bullard Arm firearms machinery valued at more than $100,000 to establish a trade school for high school boys to spend half time in school and half in the shops under institute instructors.

The trustees voted to accept when a minimum of $100,000 was obtained to establish and maintain a school on a self-supporting basis. Col. E. J. Russell offered to raise the money,

Stephen Salisbury pledged the only gift of $10,000.

Bigelow was optimistic and shipped some of the machinery to the institute. The rest was stored in a vacant building near his skating rink. The trade school plan was abandoned eventually.

In the Vienna Exposition of 1873, Bigelow had an impressive exhibit of boot and shoe machinery with which a team of shoemakers could make a pair of shoes in five minutes. When Emperor Francis Joseph saw the result of teamwork, he commented, "Were I in the shoe business, I should hate to have you for a competitor." Bigelow's Worcester competitors certainly would agree. Bigelow received the medal of progress for this exhibit.

Among other early Bigelow inventions was the gang punch to make many holes in the leather at the same time. He substituted a knife for the saw formerly used in pegging machines. At Trenton, he invented the channeling and heel-trimming machinery and used waste leather in making heels, for a more durable heel and a great saving. This improved heeling machine was his first patent. Bigelow began to patent his inventions in July 1870 on through April 1872, having patented ten shoe machines.

In 1870, he formed the Bigelow Heeling Machine Association. His machines were used in many countries in Europe and here. In 1875, after long litigation, the McKay Heeling Machine and Bigelow Heeling were consolidated as McKay & Bigelow Heeling Machine Association.

It was about this time that Bigelow handed his manufacturing to his sons for more challenging fields. He started to invest by buying properties on both shores of Lake Quinsigamond, with his characteristic energy. Worcester leaders were wary for they knew his strange ideas often controlled. Shrewsbury had mixed reactions; some were pleased and others were dismayed. In securing many acres of land on both shores of Lake Quinsigamond, he became prominent in both Worcester and Shrewsbury.

J. J. Coburn owned the Worcester & Shrewsbury Railroad, the narrow gauge steam road between the city and the lake, and land at Lake View, now called Lincoln Park in Worcester, which Bigelow bought. Coburn had begun the development of Lake View, and Bigelow continued, laying new rails, buying new cars and engines, and building an attractive station, and travel soared.

Bigelow built a summer home on the southeast shore of Lake Quinsigamond on a hilltop in 1878. This was a handsome Tudor design with a cupola on the roof, fine wood paneling, mosaics on walls and floors, and filled with antiques. It was a showplace. Unlike the Newport "cottages," which were occupied only a few weeks in the summer, Bigelow enjoyed his elegant mansion particularly when interest in his Shrewsbury property occupied his time. Close to the shore, he built a Tudor boathouse that surely was the finest on any shore.

On June 28, 1886, daughter Adelaide (Addie) Francis Bigelow married George A. Stevens in the mansion with banks of flowers, roses predominating, on the mantles and floral monograms of S and B everywhere, the bride and groom standing under "an elegant floral bell of roses" in the reception room. The bride wore a heavy white silk dress made in Paris and carried a bouquet of orange blossoms. Her brother was the best man with seven ushers. There were no bridesmaids. The grove outside was hung with electric lights as was the road to the lake powered by his mill site at a flowage dam on the northeast side of the lake, currently the site of a restaurant.

In 1882, Bigelow bought land between Worcester's Mechanic and Foster streets intending to build a handsome commercial building, but, unable to get the necessary support, he became involved with a floundering roller-skating rink. This also provided a large space as an exhibit hall.

Bigelow believed that electric power was the way of the future and, in 1883—a year before the founding of the Worcester Electric Light Company—built the first electric light and power station in Worcester to illuminate the rink. In 1887, he held an electrical exposition at the rink with 140 exhibits driven by electricity. An electric street car moved back and forth on special tracks, operating the first electric car in the city. He sold his plant to the Worcester Electric Light Company.

He had lived at 11 Elm Street and 7 Mount Pleasant Street in Worcester while working on his major Worcester projects, such as developing the roller-skating rink property into Bigelow Garden at No. 19 Foster Street corner of Mechanic Street, covering 115,000 square feet with a large skating rink building (Bigelow Society). He provided band concerts, with many and various attractions, to working-class families at prices they could afford. Bigelow Garden and roller-skating flourished.

Bigelow was expansive in giving to the people, disturbing the Worcester industrialists in 1867 with his profit sharing for his shoe plant employees. The R. G. Dun & Company credit report in 1878 called Bigelow "a keen, shrewd businessman, but not well regarded socially in some quarters" and, in 1882, as "a peculiar man of radical ideas in politics and religion, which make him rather unpopular" (Bigelow Society). That puts the situation mildly. He was a maverick. When he had an idea, he pursued it to completion, seemingly inspired by opposition.

In the 1880s, the big action in Worcester was at the Rink, or Bigelow Garden, as acquired and expanded by Bigelow, probably the most popular spot in Worcester. From 1878 into the late 1890s, popular entertainment included band concerts, plays, operas, pageants, expositions, led by roller skating, the craze of the time. It was expansive and affordable for the working family.

The Rink was 225 feet by 100 feet outside. Inside, it had a 70 feet by 175 feet rink, large enough for over 500 skaters. The Lalimes, Canadian skating promoters, were building a skating rink for the elite when they made a deal with James Plympton, the inventor of the modern roller skate, in 1863, who patented it in Europe and the United States and sold franchises for skating rinks. He returned to the United States to open a factory in Brooklyn, New York, in 1876, his patent having given him a monopoly on rinks. To use his skates, you had to buy a franchise.

The Lalimes opened on December 20, 1878 as a major event.

The *Gazette* reported "three chandeliers hanging from the center of the rink" lighted by kerosene and gasoline. "Professor Peter Kynock and other trained skaters guided more than two hundred wheeling skaters around the floor with few mishaps. William Field of Boston fitted the skates and kept them in repair." The skating frenzy had begun.

The Lalimes expanded to other cities, overextending themselves where they needed cash. This was in the early 1880s, and Horace Bigelow bought himself four Massachusetts rinks, including Worcester, with A. G. Lalime staying as manager.

Bigelow added a public swimming pool, a carousel, and concessions, with a handsome wooden fence for Bigelow Garden, which covered the block between Foster and Mechanic Streets.

Bigelow objected to the Plympton franchise system, believing that it ran counter to providing "wholesome entertainment for the hardworking people at prices within their reach." He and Sam Winslow of Winslow Skate Company, who had made more than twenty thousand pairs of roller skates for Plympton, decided to break the roller skate monopoly. On January 6, 1880, Plympton's patent expired, and Winslow began manufacturing roller skates of his own design. About the same time, Bigelow stopped paying franchise fees to Plympton and lowered admission prices. He allowed customers to use their own skates for a small fee. Plympton sued Winslow, losing in the US Circuit Court in Boston, then appealed to the US Supreme Court, but Winslow agreed to pay $500 for Plympton's rights as the original and only inventor of the roller skate.

On July 23, 1882, Bigelow decided to put on a free open air concert at Bigelow Garden. Union Church on Front Street complained to city hall that it was against the blue laws. Bigelow said he had as much right to entertain as pharmacists had to sell cigars and that he would have a concert the next Sunday. On July 31, 1882, the *Worcester Evening Gazette* reported a sacred concert by the Worcester Brass Band at five o'clock and a "Sacred Harmonic Concert" in the Rink at eight o'clock by the Ideal Opera Company on the thirtieth. Members of the police department, several having bought tickets, were highly visible.

The selections were all of sacred character, such as "Nearer, My God, to Thee," and the concert proceeded to the last selection "when the City Marshal Drennan notified Mr. Bigelow that he must stop the concert." Mr. Bigelow did so. It was attended by about eight hundred people and was not interrupted by police action

Bigelow, arraigned in the central district court for violating Sunday law and doing business on the Lord's Day, pleaded not guilty. The police testified, and only Col. Titus appeared for the defense asking Drennan about the sale of cigars and soda in drugstores because it appeared Bigelow was conducting the same business, pointing out that there was nothing degrading about the influences of the Garden.

The court fined Bigelow twenty dollars and costs for causing noise about which someone complained. Bigelow appealed to the superior court. His trials provided the chance to support the right of working people to enjoy themselves on the Sabbath.

He argued that if a rich man could ride a real horse on Sunday, why couldn't a poor man ride a wooden one? That seemed reasonable. The city decided not to press the case. By 1884, Sunday was the biggest day at Lake Park.

In 1884, Bigelow and Edward L. Davis donated 110 acres to the city of Worcester for Lake Park. Bigelow gave sixty acres and Edward L. Davis the balance. On July 4, 1885, Bigelow sponsored a boating regatta that drew about twenty thousand people. Attendance on weekends in 1882 soared to almost twenty thousand, who were transported on his Dummy Railroad purchased in 1883 from J. D. Coburn (Bigelow Society). Lake Quinsigamond bloomed.

The Dummy Railroad was fully loaded. Horace sold the Dummy to the street car company in 1892. The new trolley cars had increased weekend attendance at the lake from about 150 in 1870 to the 20,000 figure in 1890.

Horace turned his attention to the Shrewsbury side of Lake Quinsigamond where he would not be limited by Worcester's interference. He owned land on the south side of the main road to St. Anne's Cemetery. He then expanded on the lake's east shore to Route 20 with no objection from the town.

Apparently Massachusetts began to set regulations in the early 1900s. The Shrewsbury Town Hall has no records before 1974 when they adopted the Massachusetts standards.

Bigelow finished Shrewsbury's White City Amusement Park in 1905, which lasted until Labor Day 1960, long before building laws were enacted. It appears to have been built with few restrictions.

It had been hailed as the "Land of Fifty Thousand Electric Lights," which with all white buildings would have been dazzling. How would any small town handle an innovating entrepreneur like Bigelow who built his own electric light plant before Worcester's electric light company?

Several excellent books have been written about Shrewsbury's White City by current town historian, Michael Perna Jr. who has provided so much information in the Images of America postcard series, "Lake Quinsigamond and White City Amusement Park"; i.e., page 32 artist rendition of the park stated that the park would open on May 22, 1905, but labor disputes delayed the opening to June 18. A newspaper story on the delay added that the crowds became so impatient that they broke into the eighteen-acre park the day before it opened and had to be removed by the police. Bigelow was news whether he liked it or not.

This park bordered Lake Quinsigamond and included the lake waters such as boat rides, the "Whirl of Air Ships" ride swinging out over the water and trained diving horses, along with the usual amusement park attractions. However, it also included a roller-skating rink, a ballroom, and a stage for musical acts and later pop stars Paul Anka, Edie Gorme, etc.

There is much evidence of Bigelow's concern for the poor. The *Worcester Spy* on July 14, 1879 reported a series of three Bigelow's "Poor Children's Excursions" to be held in the Bigelow's grove in Shrewsbury. The first was for poor children between age five and fourteen in Worcester's wards 1, 2, and 3, the second for wards 4 and 5, the third for 6, 7, and 8. They were managed by Louis Friendly, 47 Main Street, and a large detail of police "whose only duty will be to care for the little ones."

The children would be picked up at the dummy station at 9:00 a.m. and returned by 5:30 p.m. Twelve to fifteen ladies would assist in distributing the refreshments which included six barrels of lemonade, over 1,500 sandwiches, large quantities of cookies and other dainties, thirty-five gallons of ice cream, and seven bushels of peanuts accompanied by toy kites.

The program included music by the French band, dancing, ball playing, swings, boat rides in the grove pool, and general picnic amusements. The first group included about forty "colored children," and the second one had two hundred more attendees than the first one. The parents were not invited. Food and money contributions were requested and received. This may well have been repeated in later years. Newspapers at that time were primarily advertisements with news item inserted, so later papers may not have included these notices.

Bigelow's interests often overlapped for he built the Oval in Worcester in 1892 between Sherbrook Avenue and Agate Avenue at Anna Street. Though built for track-and-field games, it was home for the New England Intercollegiate Games from 1893 to 1907. The first baseball team to use the Oval was the 1894 New England League

Club. Later teams using the Oval included Worcester, 1894 and 1898, New England League; Worcester Farmers, 1899 through 1900, International League; Worcester Quakers, 1901, International League; Worcester Hustlers, 1902, International League; Worcester Riddles, 1903, International League; and Worcester, 1904, Eastern Association. The last team was the Connecticut League team in 1904, which transferred to Norwich, Connecticut. The Oval held two thousand cheering fans.

The much quieter and more serene replacement is St. George's Cathedral, which has obliterated all signs of the park.

Lake Quinsigamond, or Long Pond, shared by Worcester and Shrewsbury is four miles long, between eighty and eighty-five feet, with a surface area of about 722 acres. It includes eight islands, which are mostly owned privately. Two islands are connected to land by a bridge. Drake Island, the largest, is state owned.

The lake waters empty into the Quinsigamond River in the Blackstone Valley. How opportune that Horace H. Bigelow came along with his innumerable plans to this lake between Shrewsbury and Worcester. It seemed meant to be.

However, while many of those living near the Lake from 1905 to 1960 remember White City with delight, some community leaders tend to "regret" the White City amusement park. This was true also in the early 1900s. An unidentified newspaper reported Worcester and Shrewsbury residents along with Boston summer home owners who appeared before the Committee on Harbors and Public Lands urged that Quinsigamond be made a reservation. This included Dr. Homer Gage of Iristhorpe, Conrad Hobbs of the Hobbs estate, and Henry Hutchins from Ard-na-Clachan.

The *Worcester Magazine* of February 1913 on "The Ruin or the Redemption of Lake Quinsigamond" by Conrad Hobbs quoted a three-year study of the lake reported to the legislature of 1912 (House Report 1696) on the increasing abuse and degradation with its increasing popularity, seeking its final reclamation and protection under strong control. Hobbs provided many statistics on the value of state control, such as Revere water park reclamation in 1911, but the state did not concur. This report is included in the story of the Hobbs estate.

In the *Shrewsbury Chronicle* on March 29, 2012, Perna told of a great ball in Newport held in 1893 by Mrs. William Vanderbilt in honor of her daughter Consuela, with favors made in Paris, and decorators/caterers working all summer to ready Marble House for five hundred guests, one of whom was Mrs. Horace H. Bigelow of Shrewsbury, Massachusetts, wife of H. H. Bigelow, who appears to have been as busy socially as Horace was in his activities. Mrs. Bigelow was the former Adelaide E. Buck, a second wife whom he married on June 1, 1859. She did have a position to maintain as the wife of such a hugely successful innovator, manufacturer, and leader.

Horace remained amazingly active into his eighties, and his record of death on July 3, 1911—at age eighty-four, which occurred during the first two weeks of the hottest days in one hundred years—put cause of death as acute dilatation of the heart and cerebral hemorrhage. Heatstroke could have contributed. It seems appropriate that his passing occurred during an extraordinary event.

His stamina and energy continued into his eighties, including his running in the firefighters' races, suing a lawyer who charged him $20,000 against an opponent who had paid only $2,000. Bigelow received a substantial settlement.

He was an astute businessman, who was not always liked, but his many efforts among the poor show his personal concern about their activities. Surely, he must have participated in the children's parties and enjoyed their antics with smiles and at least twinkling eyes. He actively supported the founding of the Bigelow family outings and history, which survives today on the Internet in the umpteenth generation. He fought for the rights of the working family; surely it was more than principle. He remains fascinating and an enigma.

HOBBS ESTATE MANSIONS ON GRAFTON STREET

Joseph Robins, Indian, sold 1,683 acres to John Haynes and Children on August 6, 1686. The heirs, unable to find the deed, were given a confirmation of the sale by Joseph Robins on January 21, 1701 (Middlesex Book 17, P. 353) by "Turf & Twigg" under the reign of William III of England, France, and Ireland.

In 1720, the property was subdivided into nine equal lots by mutual consent. John Sherman received the lot on Prospect Hill. What is now the Flynn house was identified by James Keyes Surveyer June 23, 1720, as the Robins Farm, including a house and lot of fifty acres (History by Harriette Eddy in August 1950.)

The 1832 Shrewsbury map show D. Monroe, Allen, and Harrington. In 1848, the last Munroe sold the land known as Robins Farm with house, barn, and shop to Levi Flagg and Munroe Winchester, who mortgaged to Sylvanus Flagg.

The Massachusetts land of Sylvanus Flagg of Vermont deeded to Nancy Flagg Winchester on July 24, 1860, (Book 629–489/92) was sold in September 1898, with "buildings thereon situated," by Executor Levi S. Winchester to Annie F. Hobbs of Boston for $5,200. Located in the southern part of Shrewsbury on both sides of town road 12 leading to Grafton, the property contained 104 acres of land between Routes 9 and 20 (Book 1590–323).

Thus began the history of the Hobbs family in Shrewsbury, Massachusetts. Annie Frances Kettell Hobbs was wife to wool merchant Warren D. Hobbs of Hobbs Taft & Company, then at 18 Matthew Street, Boston. Both Worcester born and raised, they were married and living in Worcester in 1870, where he was working as a wool merchant. The Marcus Hobbs House at 16 William Street, Worcester, Warren's family home, is on the National Historic Register.

In 1900, they lived at 313 Commonwealth Avenue, Boston, built in 1877 by architect William W. Lewis. Perhaps Annie chose Shrewsbury to be closer to Worcester or was lured by the Whittall Mill and the five million pounds of wool it used yearly for its rugs; it may have been a prime customer.

Shrewsbury property was numbered in 1899. The houses on the Hobbs property became 504 and 520 Grafton Street. The original one-over-one built in 1720, now forms a corner of number 504. It had been expanded in 1765, shown in town records as 1770.

The joists in the east part of the basement are split tree trunks. An ell was added in 1830. It had become a fine house when Conrad married Jessie Langmaid in 1906 and was given 504 as a wedding gift. He ordered plans for a renovation, which began in 1910, the period to which current owners began to restore in 1997. The Conrad Hobbs who lived in Boston had a handsome home in Shrewsbury, Massachusetts!

Annie had died in 1919 and Warren in 1922, leaving Conrad and sister, Henrietta, as trustees under the will. On June 7, 1929, (Book 2497–p.14/15), Conrad sold 504 to John Bath, John Bath & Company, Worcester, inventor of a grinding machine with a cutting tool, and spouse, Carrie M. Bath, with 3.7 acres, living there until 1936, when widower John died. Russell & Gretchen Bath bought 504 from his father's estate where they had been living with their son, Russell Jr. and two daughters. The handsome mansion remained in the Bath family until Russell Jr. sold it to Edward L. and Joyce Flynn of Flynn Trucking Plaza on Route 20, as is, on January 21, 1997 (Book 18569–320). Gretchen had lived there until she died in April 1995. Her son had built a house at 498, which she had given him.

The Flynns have largely restored 504 themselves after removing tons of polluted grounds. As a boy, Edward had roamed the property as his father was friends with the Baths and had loved it but never thought he could live there. They retained as much as they could. The electric light fixtures in the living room date to 1903; the dining room drapes date to 1910.

The second house on the property, built in 1890, became number 520. This was a farmhouse where tenant farmer, Ludwig Bergstrom, an 1895 emigrant from Sweden, ran Bummet Brook Farm for Warren and chauffeured as needed. Warren and Annie planned to build a mansion on the hill but had divided 520 into two areas, putting a wall from the front door up the center of the entrance staircase. Hall doors on the left entered the Bergstrom part and on the right the Hobbs quarters. The 1910 census listed ten people in the household; in 1930 only the five Bergstroms were listed. Bergstrom stayed until the late 1940s. Conrad deeded Bummet Brook Farm at number 520 to his son, Samuel and Ruth in 1950 where she bred Manchester terriers and "pharaoh" dogs imported from Malta into the late 1960s.

Samuel, born on May 20, 1915, was an administrative engineer at Whitins Machine Works, Whitinsville, Massachusetts, makers of textile machinery. The Samuel Hobbs sold 520 with 3.16 acres to Andrew J. and Eleanore L. Dell'Olio in July 1967, who removed the division, returning it to a one-family house. This was an ideal place for three sons aged twelve and under who could roam the large grounds between 520 and the mansion on the hill, which they could see from their front door.

Andrew Dell'Olio was administrator of the Grafton State Hospital when it closed in 1973; he saw that every employee was placed in a suitable job before he was sent to the Glavin Regional Center in Shrewsbury, according to proud wife, Eleanore.

Plans dated 1898 indicated that Warren planned a mansion that may have burned down, for the present mansion was built in 1911. The mansion was reached by a road in front of 520, now a driveway, with two 520 post boxes, the second one for the mansion. The mansion was assessed as number 518.

Conrad managed Hobbs Taft & Company in Boston until it was dissolved in 1931 (Mass. Acts of 1931, p. 1-3).

In the 1940s, he was president of the Massachusetts Committee for World Federation whose officers included Elizabeth Cady and William Stoddard, world leaders at the time. The University of Indiana's Lilly library had twenty boxes of material but no mention of Conrad.

He was active in an effort to make Lake Quinsigamond a state park, requested by many of the leading citizens in 1912. The *Worcester Magazine* February 1913 issue included Conrad's several page article on "The Ruin or the Redemption of Lake Quinsigamond," which is well-researched and articulate but to no avail. That seems to summarize his life. The obituary of his death on March 8, 1965 seemed that of a man of little note. Rather he was a victim of the time when the country was in depression from 1929.

The Hobbs family are buried in Rural Cemetery, Annie and Warren in a mausoleum in 1919 and 1922 respectively, Conrad in 1965, Jessie in 1948, Henrietta in 1953, and Samuel in 1969. Samuel's widow, Ruth Taft Hobbs, had remarried, been widowed, moved to Boylston, Massachusetts, and, on January 19, 1998, was killed by a hit-and-run driver, an illegal alien from Brazil who served only twenty-six months. She was cremated and interred in the family grave. Henrietta's husband, Major Walter Beal, Medical Corps US Army 1918, is buried in Neuilly, France.

Conrad and Henrietta, as trustees under Warren's will, sold 504 to Merle and Frances G. Bell on August 14, 1929, who lived there only about three years. On October 3, 1932, the Bells sold the mansion to Mae and Abraham S. Persky. Mae had been buying land from the Hobbs estate for years, acquiring most of the remaining acreage. A page in her handwriting lists her property assessments. Merle Bell was president/treasurer of Bell Manufacturing Company, maker of worsteds and woolens. The Bell Company closed in 1955 in Worcester well after his death in January 1936.

The Perskys owned the Worcester Knitting Company, acquired in 1923 from Wiley, Bickford & Sweet on Franklin Street, and opened their own business. In 1960 when the public library was built on Franklin, the company moved to 1 Brussels Street in the former Whittall Mills complex. Abraham died in 1969, and the Yoffie family purchased the business. William Yoffie became the trustee of Abraham S. Persky Charitable Trust on a local, national, and international level. Judith Yoffie was Mae Persky's niece.

Mae Persky lived in the mansion on the hill with nurse companion Teresa Oswalt and caretaker Owen McHugh. On July 1, 1976, about 11:30 p.m., they were awakened by three intruders in the house. Oswalt tried to call the police, but the wire had been cut. One guarded them while the other two searched the house for over two hours, gathering furs, silverware, jewelry, and three paintings bought by Mr. Persky in 1945. These were Childe Hassam's *In the Sun*, Gustave Courbet's *Shore of Lake Geneva*, and William Hamilton's *Lady as Shepherdess*. After taking $156 from McHugh's pocket, they took his keys and maroon 1968 Ford XL, which police found in Franklin on North Union Street. They left no prints. The police estimated $60,000 for stolen goods, and $45,000 was paid by the Commercial Union Assurance Companies for the loss of three paintings.

Mrs. Persky talked about the robbery for the rest of her life. No one had been injured though they had certainly been frightened, but over time, it had become the most exciting incident in her life, and she became quite philosophical and brave about the robbery.

She enjoyed the families on her property, even inviting Mrs. Dell'Olio to be her companion on a trip to Europe. She had had Eleaore Dell'Olio investigated and found her thoroughly respectable, but Eleanore did not accept because she was reluctant to leave her three young sons. She told me that she had later regretted not going with her for it would have been a fascinating trip. Mrs. Persky died in July 1979, leaving the estate to Judith Yoffie and William Yoffie.

The Yoffies lived in the mansion for about eighteen years, enjoying the handsome gardens, which were much loved by Judith.

A clipping "Rare Human Being Given a Rare Honor" shows Judith S. Yoffie receiving the Eleanor Roosevelt Centennial Award for her generous support of the city's civic, academic, and religious sectors in a one hundred-year birth tribute to Mrs. Roosevelt's support of Israel's economic growth.

In 1997, Judith and William sold their Shrewsbury property.

They secured a quitclaim deed signed by them on May 1, identified as 520 Grafton Street, conveying four parcels of land from the estate of Mae K. Persky to Shrewsbury Hills Limited Partnership subject to the covenant between the Yoffies and the Shrewsbury Planning Board for a subdivision, Prospect Hill, dated April 30, 1997.

The partnership sold the mansion with a few acres to Jeffrey and Sarah Millar, now at 42 Hemingway Street. One mailbox was removed and the driveway restored at 520. The Millars appreciate the history of the mansion and have framed several sections of blueprints of some of its special features.

The Millars are a young family who vastly enjoy the smaller property housing the mansion and other buildings, which they use for their business, Living Colors Incorporated, as having both housing and business enabled them to buy the property "as is" and restore or renovate as needed. The first need was to replace the kitchen and add a second story to the office building. Then they proceed as planned, restoring whenever possible. The result of their labor of love is an elegant mansion.

Sarah Millar treasures the mansion, saying that she can hardly wait until a daughter is married here. "Isn't this a marvelous place for a wedding?" It certainly is.

The story does not end here. Remember the robbery of three paintings in 1976? Let's fast-forward to February 24, 2008. The *Worcester Telegram* reports the recovery of three paintings by the FBI, and a federal court battle ensues as to the rightful owner. The paintings were located when Patrick Conley, a Rhode Island lawyer and developer, had them appraised. They had been stolen. He had received them from his brother William, an antique dealer, as collateral for a $22,000 loan. William Yoffie had died at age ninety on April 18, 2007. Judith was not a well eighty-six-year-old. The Yoffie estate, the insurance company, and Patrick Conley, who wanted at least the amount of his loan to his brother, were claimants.

Judith Yoffie died in March 2008 having seen only photographs of the paintings. In July 2008, a RI federal judge ruled the Yoffie estate rightful owners. The family of three sons was "ecstatic" that the family heirlooms were returned. The paintings were in the Worcester Art Museum where they were exhibited in 2009. In May 2012, two were to be auctioned off, Gustave Courbet's *The Shore of Lake Geneva* at Sotheby's in New York City on May 4, but it did not sell. Childe Hassam's *In the Sun* sold on May 17 for $1 million in the American art sale.

The saga of Prospect Hill in South Shrewsbury, the Hobbs estate, and the enterprising women and men who acquired and developed it during the past century is an amazing one that continues into the twenty-first century. Just imagine a wedding reception in a mansion; it sounds enchanting.

ARD-NA-CLACHAN,
THE MOEN ESTATE

IN 1899, PHILIP Washburn Moen sold Washburn & Moen Manufacturing Company to American Steel & Wire where he became vice president. With his thorough knowledge of the industry, the business had grown substantially (Crane "Historic Homes"). At that time, he acquired 365 acres of farm land in Shrewsbury from Old Post Road (W. Main) to the north, New County Road (Maple Avenue) to the south, 300 yards from Old Mill Road to the west, and 20 acres to the east on W. Main Street, which later became the Homer Gage Jr. Welwire kennels and cottage.

On this land, Moen built not only his handsome thirty-room Tudor Mansion, named Ard-na-Clachan, but also an outstanding commercial farm, which would be self-supporting in five years. The Gaelic "Village on the Hill" aptly described the hamlet of cottages for estate workers built behind the mansion while honoring his Scottish wife, Margaret Struthers Brown, whom he married in Edinburgh, Scotland, on June 5, 1890. After graduating with honors from Yale, Moen spent two years studying wire making in Sweden and traveling on the continent for a year before joining the company in 1881, first as a director, then as treasurer, and, finally in 1888, acting as general manager.

Designed by architect Ward Park Delano II and built by Shrewsbury building contractor Joseph Vaudreuil, Ard-na-Clachan was completed in 1902, the year Moen retired at forty-five from American Steel. Two years, later he died of a stroke on September 12, 1904. His widow, with three small children, ran the farm for two more years, then sold the property to Charles Henry Hutchins. On Knowles's death in 1890, Hutchins took over operation of the firm. In 1897, he bought out Crompton Loom Works, becoming Crompton & Knowles, the finest fancy loom firm in the world, He remained president until his 1917 retirement.

Francis Knowles, married twice, had children from both unions, leaving Eliza with a full brother and several halves, one being Lucius Knowles who succeeded Charles as president of Crompton & Knowles in 1917. He died in 1920. His home Knollwood in Worcester is now the Notre Dame Academy.

Eliza's half sister, Mabel Knowles, married Dr. Homer Gage, chief surgeon at the old Memorial Hospital. In 1907, the Gages bought the 138 acre Flint Farm on West Main Street, which they named *Iristhorpe*. Dr. Gage was president of Crompton & Knowles from 1920 until his death in 1938.

The Hutchins had a son, Arthur, born in 1878, and a daughter, Helen Mabel. Mother Eliza died in 1898 at 50. Charles lived in Ard-na-Clachan for fifteen years, from

1907 to November 14, 1922, when he died at seventy-five. He had continued as a gentleman farmer, retaining herds of cattle, native game and deer. In 1921, he introduced a prize-winning herd of Guernsey cow, which would remain until auctioned off in 1964.

Charles provided homes for both children. When Helen married Albert Stratton, treasurer of the Worcester County Institute for Savings, in 1912, Hutchins gave the couple an imposing Georgian-style house fronting Maple Avenue, about a mile west of the mansion, which she sold as remarried Helen H. Lindsey to Henry Hovey in 1926. Her plan of land showed twelve and one third acres west of the old estate to Old Mill Road.

Henry Prescott Hovey was an enterprising Worcester man who, at age nineteen, with his brother/partner George Russell, age seventeen, opened a laundry business. Henry had made his plans when he was in high school to learn the business at his uncle's plant, Parsons Laundries. The new plant called Hovey Laundry Company began at 2 Fruit Street, Worcester. Within five years, they were employing twenty-five people and bought land at 41 Austin Street in 1905 to erect a building specially adapted to the cleaning business.

By 1928, the building, extended through to Chandler Street, had risen to four stories completed with the most modern equipment. The Hoveys had three hundred employees, forty delivery trucks, and served a region within a radius of twenty-five miles. Henry P. and his wife, Ethel Mary Howland, descended from John Howland of the "Mayflower," had earned their mansion, one of the most beautiful in Shrewsbury. This brick Georgian with chimneys at each end had a Palladian three-part plan with a central exit into the gardens. Both ends of the building have three eight-over-eight center panel windows with an Adam-centered keystone lentil.

The front has a centered panel door with an elliptical clear fanlight and sidelights. An ell extends at right angle to the building at this central section. The central hall features a handsome double staircase and provides ventilation through the rear door set between marble pilasters directly opposite the front door. It had second level balconies on each side, overlooking the gardens. H. P. lived on his estate for eighteen years. In 1944, there was a major change.

A new enterprise came to Shrewsbury. Started at Clark University in 1944, the Worcester Foundation for Experimental Biology, founded by Drs. Hudson Hoagland and Gregory Pincus, soon needed land for this enterprise. They saw and purchased Henry Hovey's splendid home and fourteen-acre site. The records in the UMass Medical Library provide the monetary details. Minutes of special meetings of the trustees beginning in August 1944 show disbursements to date for Henry Hovey to exercise option (July 21, 1944) and for purchase of property (August 1, 1944). Others record the purchase of the Hovey property for $26,500; alterations and repairs by J. P. Lowell Incorporate of $9,310, and purchase of new equipment such as freezing units, centrifugal extractors, etc., estimated at $14,990, totaling $50,000 for the foundation's administration building. Now the Stoddard House for donor Harry Galpin Stoddard introduces another outstanding person, who was an office boy at Washburn & Moen, became president of Wyman Gordon Company and owned in partnership with journalist George W. Booth of the *Worcester Telegram*.

From the 1930s into the 1950s, these were gangbusters of Worcester Mafia boss Frank Iaconi and Providence mob leader Raymond Patriarca, who operated openly with corrupt police in both cities. Stoddard and Booth reported every activity of both, fearlessly. They also saw the need for a grass roots citizen group to change the form of government. They found a West Side Group, the Greenbriar Lane Improvement Association, later Citizens Plan E Committee, who proposed a charter change from a weak mayor, bicameral council with ten aldermen, thirty council elected by wards, and one alderman at large to a city manager and nine man council elected by proportional representation. They needed a petition with nine thousand names. The *Telegram's* 1947 front-page story named the person in each ward collecting the signatures, followed the next day by how well Cambridge was doing under Plan E. In three months, they had 12,464 signatures.

Stoddard and other top men contributed heavily to Citizens Plan E. The turnout on November 1947 election day was 72.5 percent, in favor of Plan E, 40.483 percent to 21.640 percent. Selecting the right people was essential to defeat the mafia. One told of being approached by the Mafia, but all others denied it; the paper watched the process tensely. The key was the city manager. Plan E supporters wanted an outside experienced person; the city council wanted a local. The compromise was Everett F. Merrill, a popular local businessman committed to good government. He hired Francis J. McGrath as his assistant. Fifteen months later, McGrath took over and served for thirty-five years. McGrath pleased Stoddard whose paper gave strong editorial support.

To return to Worcester Foundation, the mansion's kitchen became a lab where experiments were conducted by a brilliant young biologist, Dr. M. C. Chang, son of a

Chinese magistrate, who had been lured by the foundation's Dr. Pincus in March 1945 to come from England's Cambridge University to work here one year for $2,000. He would live in the mansion, use the kitchen lab, and double as night watchman, as the foundation had little money, and all shared in the needed labor. Dr. Chang was to stay in Shrewsbury for forty-six years.

Dr. Chang had a bachelor's degree from Tsinghua University in Beijing when he and a friend learned of two scholarships available in Great Britain, one in animal psychology, the other in animal husbandry. They flipped a coin, and Chang won animal husbandry, about which he knew nothing. He found books in English on the subject in Shanghai and stayed at a Taoist monastery to master both English and animal husbandry. He "aced" the exam and found his field. This early source has the ring of truth, but later versions differ.

He studied agricultural science for a year at Edinburgh University but accepted an invitation from Arthur Walton to research ram spermatozoa with him at Cambridge University, which he accepted. In 1961, Cambridge awarded him a PhD in animal breeding based on his many observations on testicular cooling. While researching in Amsterdam in 1939, he received a call to return to China or Cambridge immediately as World War II had begun. He chose Cambridge to continue his life work.

Most of his research at the Worcester Foundation was animal husbandry except for the few years with Dr. Pincus working on a birth control pill and in vitro fertilization for human use. When asked later about the pill, he mumbled, "They should use more water." Could this be a reference to cold showers?

He became close friends with Drs. Thomas Hunter and Edith F. Jewel, parents of Mrs. Judith McCann, physicians who served patients in Worcester and Shrewsbury, to whom Chang willed personal letters. Mrs. McCann's son Hunter is Chang's godson. Chang was playful with children but not his own, particularly his son, Poncho, reverting to the Chinese standards of his traditional family. He was a Confucian scholar with strict discipline of family and self and male dominance, which his wife, Isabelle Chin, twenty plus years younger, born in Boston, educated as librarian and writer, accepted though she wished to be partner in his work.

He loved to travel, usually as invited speaker, where he was noted for his sense of humor, with quick wit and repartee, and could be mischievous and fun-loving. He defined the Japanese as his best students for their hard work ethics, particularly Ryuzo Yanagimachi at the foundation, of whom he was most proud.

He was always generous with praise for those working under his direction. A complex man of two cultures, born in 1908 in a traditional China, he considered work essential to him, and so did his family, but with others, he could play. He died in 1991 at age eighty-one.

The foundation became a valued addition to UMass Medical School in 1997. The Stoddard House is the Regional Science Resource Center, a collaboration with Massachusetts school teachers/administrators and Worcester Foundation scientists. It serves 133 districts across the Commonwealth. Its purpose is to raise achievement levels of all students in science and math, including work in Stoddard House labs.

The house built for Charles Hutchins is the charming Spanish-style house at St. John's High School done by Worcester's leading architectural firm, Lucius Briggs & Company by Charles Briggs.

For one dollar, Charles Hutchins deeded ninety-eight acres of the north part of Ard-Na-Clachan fronting Main Street to Arthur and had a stonewall erected to separate the two properties. Arthur's house, built in nine months, was completed in December 1914.

The single-story house with its green-tile roof and spacious basement the size of the main floor consisted of three bedrooms with fireplace and connecting baths, a large living room, enclosed sun porch, a dining room, kitchen and pantry, and servants' quarters. The buzzer system to summon servants was located in an "annunciator," a glass enclosed panel on the wall in a small foyer, accessed by a buzzer located under the dining room rug. A double-tiered radiator within the pantry was used as a plate warmer. The attic over the kitchen provided storage and pull-out drawers.

The house was entered through a cloister-like columned courtyard with an inlaid brick walkway, a fountain, and a small pool. A sunken flower garden and goldfish pond lay at the bottom of the steep hill beyond the sun porch. There was a carriage house located across the graveled oval driveway from the kitchen entrance. A wooden boardwalk led from the carriage house to the residence, continuing to a gate in the stonewall of the Ard-na-Clachan property.

A treelined gravel driveway led from the West Main Street entrance to the main house. Arthur Hutchins was somewhat eccentric. A member of the Crompton & Knowles board of directors, he had little interest in business. He raised cocker spaniels, exotic birds, and other animals. His carriage house had a glass roof installed as an aviary, and a large bird case was attached to the outer wall. The foundation of the cage now supports the greenhouse, which was built in the early 1980s. A pheasant run was built by the blueberry patch to the right of the bedroom wing. Behind the house, cages were set up for various animals.

When his father died in 1922, Arthur left Shrewsbury, his house remaining vacant for three years. He joined Rollins College in Winter Park, Florida, founded in 1885 by his grandfather Francis Knowles and Congregational Ministers to "bring the educational standards of New England to the Florida frontier." There he found his calling.

Arthur taught music and voice at Rollins College. At his death at seventy-eight on October 6, 1956, he was a retired director of the music department. Rollins College annually bestows the Arthur Knowles Hutchins Scholarship to assist music students.

During this time the ownership of Ard-na-Clachan, his father's estate, changed hands. When Charles Hutchins died in 1922, Ard-na-Clachan consisted of the mansion, 112 acres between Maple Avenue and West Main Street, and ninety acres on the north side and foot of West Main Street hill, which Mr. Hutchins had obtained in a 1908 land swap with the city of Worcester. The estate was purchased in the mid-1920s for $75,000 by Howard Brewer, president of Brewer & Company of Worcester, becoming the Brewer estate. Mr. Brewer was forty years old and he, his wife Flora, and son Edwin lived here for more than forty years.

In October 1962, Mr. Brewer made an amazing sale.

The Worcester Foundation needed to expand. Already occupying the west section of the Moen property, why not extend their lands to the east, to the Brewer Mansion? Mr.

Brewer was willing to consider selling land but not the mansion. An agreement was reached in 1962 for the land, but Mr. Brewer stipulated that he and his family could live in the mansion for another ten years, which was granted. Mrs. Brewer died in 1963, Mr. Brewer in 1966. Edwin and his family stayed in the mansion until 1972.

In October 1971, the foundation, considering the use of the mansion, had three alternatives: 1) renovate and convert the upper two floors to quarters for guests attending conferences on campus and the first floor for a private club for members, with additional recreational facilities; 2) demolish and construct a new conference center on its site; and 3) demolish and use as grazing land for experimental animals.

An architect would provide costs of renovation, maintenance, and demolition, while the foundation would explore the factors involved in operating a private club by visiting selected sites to learn size of membership, dues, services, staff requirements, tax status, etc. Dr. Federico Welsch, associate director, and Roger L. Campbell, manager of development, would conduct the study. This was done and found to be impractical for the hospitality business is a far cry from the science of biology.

In September 1973, WFEB offered the town a long-term lease, rent-free, for a community use compatible with foundation work. After deliberation and referral to the Town Finance Committee, the town decided not to acquire the property, and the mansion was razed in September 1974. The determining factor was cost.

On June 2, 1926, the former Arthur Hutchins's house on West Main Street was sold for $30,000 to Mr. Richard Cleveland, president of Smith-Green Company,

Worcester, first a retail meat and grocery, then a lime and cement business.

The Cleveland family, including two sons, lived on Main Street for fifteen years, spending some time in a winter home in Nassau and at Eagle Island, Maine, in the summer. The black and white photographs on the walls of the manor house today date back to the Cleveland residency.

Richard Cleveland died in 1938. His widow stayed in the house for another three years. On May 1, 1941, the property was deeded to Mr. and Mrs. Clifford B. Sweet who subsequently named the estate *Dunmorlan*, Scottish for dune, moor, and land.

Mr. Sweet, vice president of Brewer & Company, was married to Mary Brewer, whose brother Howard had purchased Ard-na-Clachan eighteen years earlier. For a second time, the two properties were joined by a common boundary and a family tie: first father and son, now brother and sister.

The Sweet family lived at Dunmorland for fourteen years during which the 1953 tornado hit it savagely at a right angle, breaking windows, ripping off roof tiles, and toppling a corner bedroom chimney onto young Si Sweet's car parked in front. Mr. Sweet sold the property to the Xaverian brothers in June 1955. For the next seven years, the brothers lived in the main building and carriage house, commuting by car to the Temple Street High School in Worcester. A new brothers' residence was attached to the Saint John's High School in 1962.

From 1964 to 1968 the manor house was the Xaverian Brothers Juniorate, a house of formation for the young men of high school age interested in religious life. The manor house was an ideal choice for vocations with a high school on site. The sun porch served as the chapel; the main living room was a recreation room, and the three bedrooms in the main house and smaller rooms in the carriage house provided sleeping quarters.

When the Juniorate building was built in 1965, the present Flavian Hall, the manor house was used as a chapel and for dining. At the Juniorate closing in 1968, some rooms were used for small language classes, part was converted to a darkroom, and for the school's newspaper and yearbook offices.

The carriage house served as a student lounge but, since the mid-1970s, provided garage space for storage of trucks, plows, and snow removal equipment.

During 1978 and 1979, Brother Conal authorized an extensive renovation of the main floor under the supervision of Mr. Albert Etre. The kitchen was completely modernized and the other rooms were gutted, repainted, rewallpapered, and rewired. Every effort was made to retain the original atmosphere and charm of the building.

The manor house has been a vibrant part of Saint John's as the alumni office, conference rooms in the former bedroom wing, with the main room used for religious retreats, Jazz Ensemble rehearsals, Model United Nations sessions, and other student group meetings. The Drama Club and Spring Show stage crews utilized the basement space for scenery construction and storage. The manor flourished as a function hall for various outside groups and families looking for an elegant setting for banquets and parties. The yearly highlight for the manor was the Mothers' Guild Christmas Reception each December. The holiday decorating effort was the closest return to the manor's opulence, ambiance, and beauty of an earlier era in its history. In 2011, it became the retirement home for the brothers.

Only the homes Hutchins built for his two children remain of the original Ard-na-Clachan estate, but what a glorious era Philip Washburn Moen began in 1899.

HEBERT CANDY MANSION

EDMUND ELDRIDGE HILLS built his Tudor field-stone and stucco mansion, Hillswold, in 1914, as a summer residence, having bought the land in 1913 from Daniel C. Pulman. He bought more land in 1914 and 1920 from Carl E. and William H. Carey and Edwin H. Crandell, for a farm across the road.

Hillswold had thirty-two rooms with a ballroom downstairs and a back porch. It had woodwork of imported Italian pecan, canvas ceilings, and marble light fixtures. Stones used to build the house came from the property. Across the road was a farmhouse, barn, dairy, and prize English sows.

Hills was Hills and Nichols, Wool Merchants, on Summer Street in Boston, when he bought the Shrewsbury property. The May 30, 1908, issue of *Fibre & Fabric: A Record of Progress in American Textile Industries* reported that Hills and Nichols had leased the Pocasset plant of the Pocasset Combing Company to process high grades of worsted tops under the name of the Providence Combing Company, "having equipped it with all new machinery." He operated it from Boston until 1927 when he moved from Newton, Massachusetts, to Providence, Rhode Island.

The stone core of the mill was part of the 1835 Eagle Mill, becoming the Lawton Spinning Company in 1898, Pocasset Combing in 1903, and Providence Combing Mill in 1921.

Hills retired in 1940. The building is now an arts and craft center. Hills, born in Malden, Massasuchetts, April 5, 1870, had lived in Newton, Massachusetts, for many years, before coming to Providence. He had married Mabel Stuart Dorr and lived in Newton, Massachusetts, in 1902.

They divorced in 1936, and he married Mrs. Dorothy A. Howes, whom he had met in Providence, Rhode Island. He had lost interest in his Shrewsbury property and apparently never lived there according to Russell Bath Jr. who, with other children, had played in the deserted mansion as a child.

Hills conveyed the mansion to realtor Marvin Randleman on December 26, 1942 (Book 2876, 177–182), who in turn sold it to Thomas and Clara St. Pierre. The St. Pierres sold the mansion to Frederick Hebert in 1946 who established the Hebert Candy Mansion, using the ballroom for packing and the back porch as an ice cream parlor but retaining the woodwork, canvas ceilings, and marble fixtures. Various additions were made to the building as the business prospered. Hillswold's future was ensured as the famous Hebert Candy Mansion.

Frederick (Pepere) had started Hebert's Candies in his garage in 1917 when he purchased a copper kettle, knife, thermometer, table, marble slab, and stone for eleven dollars, which this enterprising man turned into an outstanding chocolate business. Pepere and his sons Gerald and Raymond opened nine retail stores in New England and shipped candy around the world.

Opening the first roadside candy mansion where customers could watch the chocolate production through a glass wall was a masterstroke of marketing. When Frederick (Pepere) Hebert died in March 1978 in his eighty-first year, he left a dynasty.

For over fifty years, Hebert's Candies flourished. Gerald's family, Richard, Frederick, Ronald and Dianne, introduced a highly profitable fundraising line and business, selling millions of candy bars in organizations here and in Canada.

The marketing world changed. The St. Pierres sold the property and Hebert sold the company to Peter Perkins of Sabrosa Foods Incorporated in 2003. The Heberts remained the first year, Fred as vice president of sales for the high volume division, Ron in product development, his wife Jeanne in marketing, each dropping out until Fred left in about fifteen months The Heberts and Perkins did not "share the same ideals"; the Heberts envisioned a tourist site, and Perkins did not.

Perkins sold the fundraising line to a Canadian company and, by 2005, had reduced staff from seventy-five to less than ten. In March 2006, the Bank of America foreclosed, and Hebert Candies was sold to a group of investors called Hebert Confections, LLC. The mansion and nine acres were sold at auction in April 2006 to Francis Polito as a long-term investment for the town.

The main investor in the company, Longmeadow Capital, with Richard Steele as the managing member, believes they can build the business on the traditions and reputation of the Hebert name. He and Tom O'Rourke, CEO of Hebert Confections, run the mansion operation keeping the Hebert quality, value and traditions, and many Hebert skilled chocolate makers, with focus on a premium Fully Loaded gourmet line, while preserving the mansion. Property owner Polito considers preserving the mansion an investment for the town in a potential growth area and is happy with Hebert Confections. The future looks hopeful for this mansion.

Though the Heberts have not been involved in their candy mansion for several years, a strong Hebert tradition remains today (2014) for a recent visit to the site revealed that families continue to return each holiday to buy candies for their adult children and now grandchildren, looking upon Hebert Candy Mansion as an integral part of family tradition.

The current management, embracing the Hebert tradition and vision of being a destination, holds Kids Candy Camps in school vacations. There's cruisin' at the mansion every Thursday at 5:00 p.m., with the weather permitting, when fully restored cars "strut their stuff." One can create masterpieces at the ice cream buffet's one trip through the sundae topping bar, Candy Mansion birthday parties, which include enticements such as a souvenir birthday card photo of party guests and a Guest of Honor Poster in its cafe, with options of a clown and/or goody bags. Senior citizens have coffee and a 15 percent discount at Senior Socials on Tuesdays. Then there are family festivities and holidays. The Hebert name carries on as a "real live candy castle."

Hills built the mansion, but the Heberts gave it the luster and identity that survives to this day. The Hebert legacy lives on, and its magic remains.

IRISTHORPE

HOMER AND MABLE GAGE ESTATE (FROM POOR HOUSE TO COUNTRY ESTATE)

"HISTORY OF THE Town of Shrewsbury from its settlement in 1717 to 1829, including Family" by Andrew W. Ward: Daniel Howe owned land on which son Gotham built house c1752 which became Flint House after Dr. Edward Flint married Daniel's daughter Mary in 1758. Daniel owned both sides of W. Main from the center of town to the bottom of the hill.

The family register shows Capt. Daniel Howe, son of Josiah, born May 3, 1681, died Nov. 22, 1768. The registered children were: Daniel, Gotham, Nathan, Gideon, Mary. Gideon Howe lived on the place now improved for the support of the town's poor. d. 1815 ("History of Worcester County").

Daniel Howe settled in North Quandrant and kept a tavern on the Great Road where Shrewsbury Poor House stood (map of 1832), on land now belonging to Mr. George H. Harlow. Dr. Edward Flint, 1733–1818, arrived in Shrewsbury c.1756. He served in French Revolutionary Wars and was a surgeon in 1775 at Cambridge. He lived with George H. Harlow and his wife, who was Dr. Flint's granddaughter.

The back half of the house had been the Howe Tavern in 1722, per license in the Shrewsbury Historic Society. In 1800 Major Josiah Flint lived in the homestead.

This is the background of the Flint property, which a century later, in 1907, was purchased by Dr. Homer Gage and his wife, Mabel Knowles Gage, of Worcester. Dr. Homer Gage, a brilliant surgeon at Worcester City Hospital, helped to establish St. Vincent Hospital and Memorial Hospital and was astute in business and financial matters.

Mabel was the daughter of Frances Bangs Knowles, cofounder of L. J. Knowles & Bros., loom manufacturers, forerunner of Crompton & Knowles, and the finest fancy loom concern in the world. Knowles was also a cofounder with Congregational Ministers in 1885 of Rollins College in Winter Park, Florida, to bring the educational standards of New England to the Florida frontier, which his descendants actively supported. Dr. Gage was president of Crompton & Knowles from 1920 to his death on July 3, 1938. The Gages had been married since June 15, 1893.

The Gages owned both sides of Main Street, Mabel the north and Dr. Homer the south side.

Mabel and Dr. Homer created the elegant Iristhorpe, a magnificent estate on Main Street. Its 138 acres included the c1752 Flint House, which they planned to replace, but having been seduced by its history and age, they moved it back fifty feet, restored and enlarged it to a handsome mansion, which became the centerpiece of an exquisite garden and estate.

The Gage's renovated house had a large dining room, three living rooms, two oversize porches, three master bedrooms, four servant rooms, and a spacious ell for the kitchen area. The landscape was designed by Mrs. Gage and her school friend, Henrietta Marquis Pope, a graduate of the Lowthorpe School of Landscape Architecture and a leading landscape architect. The gardens were extensive and exotic, including a Japanese garden and teahouse. Ground excavated for the unbuilt new house became a sunken garden. There were moonlight gardens of white flowers, rock gardens using rocks from the estate, a thirteen-acre pasture, wildflower and tulip gardens, with irises and the fleur de lis displayed everywhere. An unobstructed view of Mount Wachusetts had been created on adjoining property lined by trees to frame the vista. All of this was shared often with the public and featured at floral displays in horticultural shows in New York, Boston, and Worcester. It was the first private swimming pool.

Iristhorpe, the Iris village, included other superb buildings such as a Georgian-style four-car garage with a four-room apartment, an elegant coach stable for horses, and a two-horse sleigh in which Mrs. Gage, in white fur robes, would be driven. There was also a farmhouse, a greenhouse, and three barns built in 1915. All of these later became handsome residences.

The old coach house at 491 Main Street became the home of horticulturist Allen Jenkins from Straffordshire, England, who came to the United States in 1900, oversaw with a twelve to eighteen crew the incredible Iristhorpe gardens for thirty-five years and lived in Shrewsbury for forty-seven years.

Iristhorpe seemed like a paradise, but the Gages also had a great sorrow when their only son Homer died on September 2, 1925 at age thirty of polio. Homer had begun a dog kennel in 1921 in the one house on the south side, 460 Main Street, Lot 6, which appears to be the original house and kennels built by Phillip Washburn Moen c1902. Dr. Homer acquired the land from Henry Hovey who had bought the house with twelve acres given to Helen Hutchins by her father when she married. Homer had a highly successful dog kennel, Welwire, where he bred wire-haired and Welsh terriers assisted by his British kennel master, Joseph Booth and his wife. Welwire was noted for its many winning champions. The year before, he had written a letter requesting that the kennel be maintained with an endowment for the life of the kennel master if anything happened to him. The Gages, finding the letter, honored his wishes.

A fire on April 2, 1931 raced through the stalls of champion show dogs, destroying twenty-eight dogs; only one of the top winning wirehaired terriers remained among the seventeen dogs that survived. Many were international champions. While some were burned; most were suffocated. The loss was inestimable, as the dogs were among the top dogs in American Kennel Club lists as winners. A $90 to $100,000 estimate in the clipping was just a minimum guess.

Mr. Booth, the kennel master, had been in Worcester for the evening, returning with Mr. Terry Bresnahan, a painter of dogs who often visited, a few minutes after the fire broke out. While Bresnahan called the fire department at about 2:45 a.m., Booth smashed a window to enter the frame building to release the runway but was driven back by intense heat and smoke. It ended a breeding line that was priceless. The last dog bred by Homer Gage was an older dog, Hafran Wizard, whom the Gages prized beyond dollars.

Fire Chief Edward A. Logan reported that the fire started from an overheated furnace in the basement. The kennel master's home and part of the kennel in the rear, now a workshop, can still be seen.

A warm caring person, Mabel Gage adopted several French war orphans and gave to many charities in France and here until her death in 1948. Dr. Gage had died on July 3, 1938, willing his land to her. Her will provided for her orphans and charities as well as those who had contributed to her beautiful Iristhorpe.

She specified that all the property be sold but fifty acres of woodland to be shared by all and kept in its present state.

Mabel Knowles Gage had gifted Rollins College, cofounded by Francis Bangs Knowles, with the French House and its maintenance in 1941. Her will provided $50,000 toward the maintenance of the French House and its director "as the trustees shall deem necessary or advisable, and thereafter for the general purposes of said college."

Allen Jenkins was left $20,000, the old coach house and land at 491 in appreciation of his years of dedicated service.

The integrity of his pre-1840 house has been retained, showing three distinct historical periods from before 1840 even to the attached privy ell, now used for storage.

Josiah Flint sold this house to Eli Wolcott, a Worcester shoemaker who had married Mary Flint. A federal-style, it has a Palladian window and a main entrance at the gable end. The Flint farm included the Wolcott buildings.

In 1908, Mable Gage hired Jenkins who was president of the Lenox Horticultural Society in the Berkshires. Jenkins was an established and respected horticulturist who held offices in the Worcester County Horticultural Society and the National Association of Gardeners, serving as president in 1933 while overseeing Iristhorpe. He was a member of the Worcester County Horticultural Society for forty years, a former trustee, a director for ten years, and chairman of the exhibit arrangement committee for many years.

While overseeing the Iristhorpe gardens and thereafter, the flower displays shown in Worcester, Boston, and New York horticultural shows, Jenkins won numerous cups and trophies for both Mrs. Gage and himself.

Jenkins was chairman of the Park Commissioners here for thirty-five years, a deputy fire chief for thirty years, a former trustee of Mountain View Cemetery, and a town meeting member from Precinct 1. None of the awards have been recovered and may have been destroyed in a bonfire when his daughter prepared the house for sale. His was an active life as a horticulturist for and with Mabel Gage in creating her superb grounds and exhibits.

In June 1962, his daughter/executor Doris French sold the property to Robert Burgess, the penultimate president of the A. E. Burgess and Hickey Leather Companies, the tannery and currying business begun in Shrewsbury in 1798 to 1799 at the corner of Main and South Streets, which remained until 1946, when it was moved to Grafton. During the Burgess residency, the four rooms in the rear on the second floor were rented out from 1971 to 1974. The following year, the Burgesses left Iristhorpe, selling it on October 1, 1975 to Maurice J. and Pamela K. Boisvert, its present owners.

In April 1950, the *Worcester Evening Gazette* listed the following buyers: Harold G. Clayton, Supt., Bay State Abrasive of Westboro, buying the Gage mansion and thirty-two acres including the Japanese garden and teahouse. He handled the sale of Iristhorpe to Albert H. Taylor, Webster industrialist, who bought the Coach Stable and eight acres; Joseph R. Carter, vice president/general manager, Johnson Steel & Wire of Worcester, bought the Georgian-style garage and eight acres; James A. Smith, president/treasurer, C. K. Smith & Co., Worcester, bought thirteen acres of pasture land west of the main house; H. Craig Hill bought the farmhouse, greenhouse, 1915 barn; Warren H. Howard, sales manager, General Electric, bought the sunken garden and two acres where he could build a residence.

Paul Perreault bought water tower and two acres fed by artesian well with attached 1908 filter house and twenty acres between Main and Maple Avenue to develop Hillcrest of seventy-two houses to be designed by Harry Morgan. Allen J. Jenkins, having inherited the old coach house, bought an acre to square out the land.

Some of the current owners have shared stories about this cherished community that retains its graciousness though with modest grounds. The past sixty-odd years have been gentle to Iristhorpe. The original house, coach house, garage, and head gardener's house remain as charming residences.

The farmhouse, 1915 barn, and greenhouse were razed in September 2009 to be replaced with a large ranch house. Having been bought by H. Craig Hill, it was home to Warren and Marian Higgins from October 1959 to their deaths in 2006 and 2007, respectively. Marian's niece inherited and sold it in 2009. The properties built in the 1950s on Iristhorpe gardens retain generous grounds.

The year after Mabel Gage died, the *Worcester Telegram* on June 7, 1949 wrote that "More than five thousand persons yesterday roved over the Iristhorpe estate of the late Mrs. Homer Gage," prior to the two-day auction held in a large tent on the grounds of Iristhorpe and her Worcester home at 8 Chestnut Street consisting of more than one thousand lots of household furnishings.

The Boston auctioneer said that "the preview crowds" have been the largest he has ever seen. This was a famous eastern estate for some forty years with one hundred acres of magnificent gardens. In June, its thirty-two acres of multicolored iris surrounding the mansion were in full bloom as were its many other gardens.

It even included a miniature merry-go-round with diminutive revolving wooden horses for its small riders.

The coach stable held carriages, landaus, broughams, gigs, and sleighs, which were to be sold. Other yesteryear items were for sale, such as ostrich feather boas, French parasols, and bronze Rogers statue groups, a feature of every genteel home of the era.

Although all the Iristhorpe buildings were sold and became residences, this is the story of the original two old houses—the Flint house, which became the Gage mansion at 449 Main, and the c1840 Eli Wolcott house, which Josiah Flint sold when Eli married Mary Flint at 491 Main—and the old Ard-na-Clachan kennels and house across the street at 460 Main Street where Homer Gage Jr. housed his kennel.

The Flint house purchased by Harold G. Clayton in 1950 was sold on November 23, 1960 to Paul S. and Anne M. Morgan.

On Dec. 13, 1970, the Morgans were returning from Europe.

Their caretaker, Rocco Zecco, mowed the grass Saturday, returning at 5:00 a.m. Sunday the thirteenth to finish the mowing. Zecco smelled smoke on entering the drive, parked in front, ran to open the rear kitchen door, and was driven back by intense smoke and heat. He drove to the fire station. On his return, he saw flames in the bay window on the east side of the kitchen.

"Nine fully equipped firemen found the kitchen, floor above, and the cellar fully charged with fire, which spread vertically and horizontally over the building, destroying all of the wiring in the vicinity.

"The fire, originating in a cedar closet in the cellar, burned it, the ceiling and walls, spread along the vent pipe through to the attic above kitchen area, followed the roof line to attic in front of house, then through the roof. The kitchen ell was destroyed" (Fire report).

The Morgans were insured and remained in the house until they sold to the current owners, the Malcolm Morvilles, on December 21, 1993.

Allen Jenkins achieved a full, successful life in his field of horticulture, including the magnificent Iristhorpe gardens, a truly joint effort of Mabel Gage and Allen Jenkins. She was the dreamer, and he helped to fulfill her dreams. Between them, they left a legacy.

Jenkins died February 1962 at age eighty-one.

The Worcester County Horticultural Society records at Tower Hill show the key role it played in the late nineteenth and early to mid-twentieth centuries in Shrewsbury and Worcester. Jenkins joined in 1915, while both Gages joined in 1917 as Worcester residents. Mrs. Gertrude Whittall joined in 1919 though Matthew Whittall had been an active member since 1875, winning many awards for his exhibits.

Jenkins, Mrs. Homer Gage, and Mrs. Whittall were all trustees in the 1918–1919 Transactions. In 1920, both Allen

J. Jenkins and Mrs. Gage were trustees, and Jenkins was a member of the Arrangements and Exhibit Committee. In 1926, Jenkins became chair of Arrangements and Exhibit Committee, remaining so until 1951 to 1952 when he was listed as honorary chair until his death.

He remained active on several other committees. Both Iristhorpe and its horticulturist regularly won prizes for their exhibits. Jenkins most prized award was the large gold medal from the Massachusetts Horticultural Society in 1930. Although listed fourth in order of value, it is the highest award given for garden exhibitions of unusual merit to garden superintendents for "Skill in Horticulture" as a professional horticulturist.

Despite having won numerous cups and trophies, this had the greatest meaning as it placed him at the top of his profession.

WHITTALL MANSION JUNIPER HALL AND MASONIC HOME/HOSPITAL

MATTHEW JOHN WHITTALL, president of the Whittall Mill, the largest carpet manufacturer in Worcester, was born in Kidderminster, England on March 10, 1843. At age fourteen, he learned the carpet business at Messrs. Humphries & Sons, becoming an assistant superintendent. At age twenty-one, he joined T. B. Worth at Stourpart, in charge of the workers. He married M. Ellen Paget and had five children, with only a son and daughter surviving.

In 1870, he corresponded with Crompton Carpet Works in Worcester, Massachusetts, arriving in May 1871, remaining with them until 1879 when the company closed. In July 1880, Whittall was made a Master Mason. This was a man who wasted no time.

In 1880, Whittall began a small business in a building owned by Wicks Manufacturing Company, having purchased in England machines to make Wilton and Brussells carpets. This business grew into three large carpet mills and a worsted mill covering almost 200,800 square feet of land and consuming over five million pounds of wool per year. The firm produced not only standard patterns of Wilton and Brussells carpets but new ones designed from French and English sources and originals by his own gifted staff (Worcester of 1898, 50 years a city, public library–public domain). It closed in 1944.

An active Episcopalian, Whittall provided the Parish of St. Matthew at Worcester's Cambridge and Southbridge Streets on the opposite corner from his Worcester home, later occupied by his son when the Whittalls moved to Juniper Hall.

Whittall had attended no college and considered it no lack; as he expressed it, "Whether a man has a college education or not, it depends entirely upon himself as to his success. Some men, because of perseverance, stick-to-it natures, are going to succeed anyway. If they can't find a way around an obstacle, they'll kick a hole through it. They will either find a way or make it!"

On June 4, 1906, the sixty-three-year-old Whittall, a widower, married Gertrude Littlefield Clarke, forty-nine-year-old daughter of the Hon. and Mrs. Henry Tefft Clarke of Omaha, Nebraska, also a Master Mason. Born in New York in 1834, Clarke was only nine years older than Whittall with the same drive. In 1906, Clarke was elected president of the Nebraska Territorial Pioneers' Association and the Nebraska State Historical Society, having been a major factor in founding Bellevue, Nebraska, and the Union Pacific Railroad from Bellevue to Sioux City via Omaha. He made multiple contributions as a freighter, highway and bridge builder, merchant wholesaler, territorial legislator, and council. In 1876, he began the Clarke Centennial Pony Express connecting Sidney with the Black Hills outposts. He, too, was a man "who would find a way or make it."

Although Whittall's private papers were not found, it seems possible that they met at Masonic affairs as both Whittall and her father were thirty-third degree Master Masons. She as the only daughter, who had remained at home and unmarried, would accompany her widowed father as his hostess and companion. The wives and daughters of Masons play a prominent role in the social activities associated with the Masons, having their own Eastern Star where they become "master hostesses" equal to their husbands' and fathers' status.

In 1912, the Whittalls were ready to seek a handsome summer property. That summer Whittall purchased one hundred acres on the top of Meeting Hill Road, comprised of seven separately owned properties, and hired the Norcross Brothers to build his estate, Juniper Hall, a two-story Georgian house with magnificent gardens and a teahouse.

One of the highest and finest views in Shrewsbury, it overlooked Lake Quinsigamond and beyond to the hills of Paxton and Rutland and the mountains of Monadnock and Wachusetts.

Juniper Hall became one of the handsomest homes in the most beautiful location in Shrewsbury. Completed in 1912, as noted on its main fireplace, its rooms were large with a two-story reception room surrounded by a balcony, a music room, living and dining room, breakfast room, and the butler's pantry on the first floor. Upstairs were four bedrooms with fireplaces, and bathrooms, and a large sitting room. A sunporch faced the formal gardens, covering one side of the house. The grounds included a pool, picking flower gardens, showcase gardens, and masses of lilacs, which were open to the public at their peak.

The Whittalls were both very active in the Worcester County Horticultural Society, with Matthew since 1875. He had the largest exhibit in June of 1913 to 1914. Mrs. Whittall joined in Shrewsbury in 1919 and is listed as trustee in 1921 through 1928, proposing with Mrs. Gage of Iristhorpe the new site at 30 Elm Street in 1926.

A double house was built between the mansion and the tower to provide two homes, one for the fireman/grounds keeper and one for the chauffeur. In 1920, a baby girl was born to the Laydens, the fireman's family. She was named Mary Gertrude to honor Gertrude Whittall, the second child following two-year-old Joe and, two years later, Fred. She proudly showed the shining sterling silver baby bowl and spoon received from Mrs. Whittall.

Mary, active in Shrewsbury and St. Mary's Catholic Church, was featured in St. Mary's Parish newsletter of March 2011.

Her parents, both recent emigrants from England, met and married in Boston. They moved to Worcester where he was hired as fireman at the Whittall Carpet mill. When the Whittalls built their home in Shrewsbury, the Laydens came to Juniper Hall to live and work. When the property was given to the Masons, they moved to an apartment on Main Street on the first floor of what is now (2013) Britton's Funeral Home. Mary's father then worked at the Hickey Leather Factory at Main and South Streets, the family later moving to South Street.

It was Mary who said that Mrs. Whittall talked about a Stradivari, which revealed Mrs. Whittall's love of music and the Stradivari instruments that consumed her. First exposed to chamber music in Worcester in 1908 when the Flonzaley String Quartet performed for the Whittalls, she studied the violoncello and collected five instruments, three violins, a viola, and a cello, with high quality Tourte bows, which she presented to the Library of Congress in 1935 soon after she moved to Washington, DC

She established the Gertrude Clarke Whittall Foundation to insure they would be played in concerts by leading violinists, which included Itzhak Perlman as an eighteen-year-old violinist from Israel. He remained to become one of America's finest artists in the twentieth century.

Until her death at ninety-seven on June 30, 1965, Mrs. Whittall gave funds to the library to house the instruments, support concerts, house an invaluable collection of autographed musical scores, a poetry room, and a fund to present poets reading their works, actors interpreting Shakespeare, and critics lecturing on literature.

For over thirty years, Mrs. Whittall shared the best music and literature with the public performed by the finest musicians and interpreters. This great lady spent her wealth for the benefit of many others, thoroughly enjoying every moment.

Matthew Whittall was on the governor's council from Worcester's Seventh District under Governor Calvin Coolidge at the time of a Boston police strike which Coolidge resolved by use of the National Guard. This attracted the attention of the Republicans who selected him vice president at its convention. At this time, Coolidge visited Juniper Hall. Whittall enjoyed his superb house for only ten years, for he died in 1922 at age seventy-nine. In 1927, Mrs. Whittall deeded the property to the Masons, though she presented it formally to the Massachusetts Grand Lodge of Masons on Memorial Day 1928 in an official ceremony in honor of her husband for their use as a home and hospital for needy members and their families.

On June 13, the Grand Lodge authorized the operation of the hospital, and on June 29, three patients were transferred from the Charlton Masonic Home. It also authorized the construction and equipment of a new wing to join the northerly wing of the present house for fifty-five more beds.

Mrs. Whittall had provided a pristine house with everything in it and further supplied furniture, bedding, linens, silver and dishes for twelve patients in the hospital. Further, in 1928, she set up a trust fund with a Boston bank to provide certain life income with the principal fund to be "distributed, free of this trust 'to the Grand Lodge of Masons in Massachusetts' for the use of Juniper Hall Hospital." She was a generous and caring lady throughout her life, surpassing herself in her many years in Washington, DC.

On September 26, 1928, the Masons placed a copperbox and its contents in the cornerstone of the new $250,000 seventy-room hospital wing to Juniper Hall, Shrewsbury, and the memorial tablet of the Grand Lodge was unveiled under the porte cochere. The wing had fifty-nine beds, forty of them single beds.

The cost for patients in the hospital was charged to Grand Lodge funds or income rather than the lodge to which the patient belonged. Half of $200,000 cost for the wing was paid by the Grand Lodge, and the balance, including $50,000 for an endowment fund, was raised by popular subscription of the membership.

A bronze memorial tablet was affixed to the front wall of the house picturing Matthew Whittall and the following: His full name—"Founder of these mills—Born in Kidderminster, England, March 10, 1843—DIED AT JUNIPER HALL, SHREWSBURY—October 31, 1922—'A MAN WHOSE HEART WAS EVER-FULL OF LOVE FOR HIS FELLOW-MEN'—Presented by Mrs. Whittall in memory of her husband."

The Masons had a similar tablet as follows: "Raised a Master Mason July 19, 1880.—Worshipful MASTER–Isiah Thomas Lodge 1922—Director of the Grand Lodge, 1915–1922. Honorary J Member. Supreme Council, 33, A.A.S.R., 1922,—'A man whose heart was ever full of love for his fellow man.'"

A good employer, he paid well, took care of his employees in illness, provided safe working conditions and a playing field for their well-being, and gave them security. Indeed, he was a man full of love for his fellow man.

Juniper Hall as the Masonic home/hospital would provide complete retirement home for its members and their spouses for forty-seven years. An example of one resident was Edward H. Beauregard, born August 15, 1880, died April 12, 1972, aged ninety-two, who lived at Juniper Hall for fifteen years. His daughter, Doris Hasselton, mother of friend Virginia Ross, worked at Juniper Hall during that time. Virginia generously provided family information.

Edward, known as Gramp, one of six children, had been a plumber and steamfitter, volunteer fireman, and a Mason.

He had sired five children, four daughters and one son.

Renovations and additions were made to the home over the years to the 1970s when the decision was made in March 1972 to phase out the Juniper Hall, which was now a nursing home, and to merge Shrewsbury operations with Charlton's. Two wings were built at Charlton, increasing patients from 132 to 156, and the nursing home residents were moved to Charlton, but the Juniper Hall name would be retained through the twentieth century.

The Whittall's Juniper Hall and the Grand Lodge AF&AM of Massachusetts provided extended care for 534 patients from all their lodges and their spouses for close to five decades, from June 28, 1928, to its latest patient Russell B. Palmer, from Natick (Wellesley Lodge) who arrived August 27, 1974, one of twenty-nine patients who moved March 1975 to Charlton.

The Grand Lodge offered to sell the property to the town of Shrewsbury that year. In 1976, the town voted at a special meeting to acquire the property for $400,000. The purchase and sales agreement called for the consummation of the transaction on June 8, 1976. Town members, not able to agree on how to utilize the property, hired a care-taker to live in the house, but the land and buildings were vandalized, and the town decided to demolish the building in 1979.

Just a short distance from Main Street on Prospect Street, this could have been a community center for recep-tions and meetings, for seniors and historic groups, for all types of group activities. But it also takes dedicated peo-ple and money. As with the Worcester Foundation for Experimental Biology, it needed people with specialized knowledge of the hospitality business.

The Mason home in Charlton, now (2011) celebrating its hundredth anniversary, appears to have operated in close cooperation with Shrewsbury's Juniper Hall and, at least in its declining years, as an adjunct. In 1968, Charlton had built a two-story gable-roofed brick infirmary of twenty-one beds on a second level, calling it Juniper Hall, completed in 1969.

In 1980, the lower floor was completed bringing the nursing facility to its full capacity. This building was demolished in the early 2000s as an all new Overlook Community was built.

Charlton's story is interesting. An elegant hotel was built on the site in 1905 accessible via the Southbridge Street Railway and the hotel carriage to the hardworking Worcester industrial leaders for refreshing rest and recreation. But its tenure was brief, for within a few years, it was bankrupt due to a larcenous partner who stole the hotel's money.

A handsome building, the guest entered a welcoming foyer with a graceful center stairway, which curved on the landing to double staircases leading to the second level, an auspicious beginning for Charlton's Masonic Home.

The site of the former Whittall/Masonic home and hospital became Prospect Park, with decayed pergola/teahouse, strangled gardens, and major overgrowth.

After many years of neglect, a small group, initially part of the Garden Club, wanted to make the site accessible to the community. In 2003, the Friends of Prospect Park incorporated when others had joined and began to open up walking trails and former garden sites; clear, clean, and maintain the park; and work with others who have taken on park projects as part of a scout activity or as a school assignment or to put in a small garden.

In the spring, some self-seeded flowers pop up, areas of green ferns appear, and rampant wisteria has even strangled some of the trees. The pergola/teahouse renamed The Garden of Sweet Remembrance in honor of Matthew John Whittall remains. Perhaps one day, it could be restored as a memorial to honor and treasure the Whittall and Masonic heritage of caring for others that is unique to this site so near the center of the town of Shrewsbury.

THE HOUGHTON ESTATE

59 SOUTH STREET, SHREWSBURY

STRICTLY SPEAKING, THIS is not a mansion; however, associate Chris Kirk wanted to include this as it is an estate with a very interesting story, and it is across South Street from where I live, and one of our sources had known Allie Houghton, so it is included.

Allie Barth Houghton was born March 2, 1867, in Pettis, Missouri, to James Bascum Rhodus from Madison County, Kentucky, and Georgina Anna Yates from Louisville, Kentucky. Sometime after the birth of a brother James, born in 1869, their father, James Rhodus, left them.

Their mother next married Moritz A. Barth from Germany on January 7, 1880 in Denver, Colorado, as a widow, becoming Georgia A. Barth. Moritz Barth adopted both children, whom he loved as his own. Allie's adoption is recorded in book 27 page 508 in county of Arapahoe records, now Denver, Colorado.

Moritz and Georgia then had three children: Georgia Mable who was born in 1880 and died in 1886, Paulina who lived from 1883 to 1885, son Moritz Allen Barth Jr. who was born in 1890 in Denver. In 1903, the family moved to Boston, where they lived at the Westminster, Copley Square, enjoyed trips to Newport, Rhode Island, and spent summers at Kennebunkport, Maine. His son graduated from Harvard, received Supreme Court bar admission in 1916 and later owned the Barth Hotel of Denver.

At the time of Barth's death on June 5, 1918, Moritz Jr. was an instructor in the marine training school at Mare Island, California. He married Josephine Hooper of Denver and had a daughter Josephine.

Moritz Barth—born on July 24, 1834, in Dietz, Nassau, Germany—was son of George and Mina Barth, one of five sons and three daughters. He attended public school and gymnasium until he was age fourteen when he worked in the surveyor general's office until he decided to go to America. He then became a shoemaker and left Havre on the sailing ship *William Nelson* in 1852 to arrive fifty-four days later in New Orleans in December. He made shoes there until May when he and his brother William moved up the Mississippi to St. Clair County, Illinois, staying until 1854, then on to Parkville, Missouri, where they began a business. As union men opposing slavery, they were unwelcome in pro-slavery Missouri and moved to Colorado, where gold had been found, crossing the Missouri River on June 2, 1861, by ox-team and wagon, arriving in California Gulch near Leadville a month later. They worked in shoemaking for a few months when William returned to St. Louis and Moritz to Canon City, Colorado, where he opened a general store briefly, then rejoined William in St. Louis making shoes and boots. They specialized in heavy nail boots for the Rocky Mountain trade.

In 1862, they crossed the plains to Colorado with two wagons, one for William headed for Fairplay Park County and the second for Moritz going to Montgomery, the head of Southpark. The following spring, he went over the range to Gold Run, staying until the following autumn when Montana gold lured him, so he bought a large stock of goods to set up business in Virginia City until the fall of 1865.

He and brother William then returned to Denver, successfully set up an extensive shoe business at first in a narrow space between two buildings, then in a larger store between Market and Blake Streets at 232 Fifteenth Street. They set up branches in Salt Lake City and Corinne, Utah, returning to Denver in 1870 where both stayed until 1882 when they sold their very profitable business.

With this success and the increase in property values in Denver, Moritiz made a large fortune with the real estate he had been buying in Denver. He built the Barth Block at the corner of Sixteenth and Lawrence Streets, occupied for a time by the City National Bank of which he became a stockholder and director. He was also a director of the Denver Tramway Company and Denver Consolidated Tramway Company.

At age forty-six, Moritz was wealthy when he wed the widow Georgia Rhodus and adopted her daughter Allie and son James, so we pick up the tale of Allie Barth's rise from waif to wealth.

Allie graduated from Wellesley and married Frank Newton Houghton at the Barth home at 1773 Grant Avenue, Denver, on November 16, 1887. Her wedding dress from Paris is in the collection of the Worcester Historical Museum. She may have presented it herself for an undated note naming bride and groom, married in Denver, Colorado, is attached to the boxed gown which has never been displayed.

Frank Houghton, born April 18, 1862, was the third child of six children and the first son of Charles Chandler Houghton and Elvira Lavinia Newton, both born in Vernon, Vermont, who were married in Worcester, Massachusetts, in 1855.

Frank graduated from the Military School of Worcester at eighteen. This appears to have been the Highland Military Academy opened in 1856 by Caleb B. Metcalf in his home where Military Road and Salsbury Street meet. At first, limited to sixteen boarders and twenty day students, it was quality education with fine teachers. It was highly respected and existed for at least fifty years.

He entered his father's factory, making shoes and boots in 1880, on his graduation. In 1884, the firm was C. C. Houghton & Company, 105 Front Street, Worcester. In 1890, it became Houghton, Hibbard & Warren making shoes in Sommersworth, New Hampshire.

Frank and Allie were living at 404 Grafton Street in Worcester in 1916. They moved to Shrewsbury in 1918. They began to buy land in Shrewsbury, possibly because that had been a major source of Barth's fortune, but this was not Denver in the 1800s, though they did well.

Moritz Barth, Allie's doting stepfather, died in 1918 and would leave Allie a small fortune. They bought 59 South Street from Eliza J. Keegan on January 24, 1921, including a house. (Worcester Deed book 2235, 473, public records.)

An odd *Worcester Telegram* clipping dated April 27, 1958, reporting Allie's death mentions that she and her brother contested their mother's will in December 1929, which left about $1 million to her granddaughter, child of her son, Moritz Jr. The court ruled that the estate be placed in trust with the grandchild, Mrs. Houghton, and her brother each to receive one-third of the income. They weren't willing to share the wealth apparently. It was during the six-year litigation of Allie's mother's will that Allie learned her father's first name, James, and that he had died in Missouri on December 14, 1917.

Allie's Shrewsbury house on at least twenty-two acres looked like a Georgian-style gable farmhouse with chimneys at each end.

A front view shows two buildings attached through a covered passageway, an enclosed sunroom, and a large flower garden in the rear facing a grove of trees. These could be Houghton additions. We do know that it was forty-eight acres when it was sold to the Passionist Fathers, which would include the two parcels they had bought on Golden Hill.

A delightful source was Judith McCann, the only child of Drs. Thomas Hunter and (wife) Edith F. Jewell. Originally from Worcester, they served patients in both Worcester and Shrewsbury, and Dr. Jewell Hunter was Allie's friend and doctor who stayed with her the last week of Allie's life; Allie died in Dr. Hunter's arms.

Frank had died April 25, 1931, one week past his sixty-ninth birthday. Allie had kept his ashes in a boot on the mantelpiece in her home. She died on April 25, 1958 at the age of ninety-one. They are buried at Worcester Rural Cemetery on South Cypress Avenue.

Judith, who had enjoyed Christmas at the Houghton estate, said, "Mrs. Houghton had a joie de vivre and could relate to young people." She enjoyed Christmas and decorated for the holiday, filling a large Paul Revere silver bowl with silver dollars; young children could have two handfuls of coin, whereas older children could have only one. She sometimes visited the Hunters, provided them with box seats to the Boston Opera, and no doubt, Judith had enjoyed both the two handsful of silver dollars and the one handful each Christmas.

Allie loved her estate and signed family correspondence "Your Great Aunt Allie from Golden Hill." Golden Hill really was a hill, just a bit southwest of their street residence. The Houghtons had had no children, but many children had been Allie's friends.

Allie was a "grande dame" who rode in the backseat in her chauffeured car, graciously acknowledging her friends. In her last years, she had two Chinese houseboys, Key and Bo. She complained that the only people who visited her were those who wanted her to leave them money. It is probable that she was right about some of them. Money does attract.

She specified in her will that the estate was not to be sold to the Catholic Church. Worcester's Bishop Wright was buying large parcels of land in the region. He wasn't going to get hers. Well, he didn't—directly. Allie's executor, the Mechanics Bank in Worcester, sold the property to Cosmo E. and Elaine F. Mingolla on September 18, 1958 (Deed Book 3970, 301, public records).

On July 7, 1960, per *Deed Book 4121* on page 586, the property goes to the Passionist Fathers of Shrewsbury, Incorporated. Their Passionist Silver Jubilee book *A Celebration of Twenty-five Years* on page 10, tells all. After a six month search for a site for their center, the Passionists found "current owner and willing seller, Mr. Cosmo E. Mingolla, a Catholic businessman and retreatant" current owner of 59 South Street known as Golden Hill. The estate, 48 acres of land, had a nine-room house, a three-car garage, and a one-room camp. It really wasn't planned, Allie.

In August, the Houghton house was converted. The porch became a meeting room, the living room became a chapel for days or evenings of recollection, and a large cross was placed on the south end chimney.

From early September, Father Gilbert stayed at St. Mary's Rectory a few blocks away until the Houghton house was ready. In October, Rev. Berchmans McHugh, CP was reassigned from Brighton's St. Gabriel's Monastery. In November, he, Fr. Gilbert and Ed Mulvey, a former Navy man, as cook, moved into the house.

On November 11, 1960, the first mass was celebrated, followed by the second by Father Berchmans.

On November 23, an evening of recollection was attended by thirty-two men being inducted into the Knights of Columbus, Benedict Council 2379, Fisherville. On Christmas Eve, about thirty members and benefactors attended Midnight Mass. Daytime recollections were conducted for public high school students, and for men, and evenings for both groups and for married couples. During Lent of 1961, twenty groups of between fifteen- to forty-year-olds, including members of sodalities or social clubs, attended Evenings of Recollection. Chef Ed Mulvey was replaced by Brother Paul Joseph Morgan, CP of the Pittsburgh Community.

The priests became active throughout the diocese assisting the parishes as needed for daily mass and on Sundays for the Xaverian Brothers at the newly completed St. John's

High School on upper Main Street in Shrewsbury. In the fall of 1961, the erection of a retreat house was planned. This would require more acreage, so two small lots were bought from the town of Shrewsbury, and on November 5, 1963, five acres on the north end at 21 South Street were obtained for a total of about fifty-four acres, the house to be used until the new monastery was ready.

Fr. Gilbert selected the name *Calvary*, and the community would be the Calvary Monastery Retreat. "A retreat is a unique opportunity to reflect on one's life...for spiritual and personal refreshment." It is forty hours away from one's pressures in serene solitude for rest and reflection.

The first ecumenical retreat in April 1967 encouraged other denominations to use the retreat center. Both Lutherans and Episcopalians have held their own retreats and conferences in the facility. Monthly "Quiet Mornings for Women," formerly "Mothers' Morning Out," meetings gave quiet time for women to reflect. They held recovery retreats for the men, women, and families of those with alcohol problems, including Caring for the Inner Child for anyone affected by addictive disorders. Their Elderhostel provided educational programs for older adults in philosophy, religion, and ethics.

The words "Come to me, all you who are burdened, and I will refresh you" welcomed all who entered the center. The previous year, five thousand of both genders and all ages came to be helped.

When Lyn visited in 2008 to find out about it, a serene woman in her forties told of a young scared pregnant girl coming for help who was welcomed and assisted. The woman said they became her family and added, "I cannot imagine my life without my twenty-year-old daughter."

The Calvary Guild, a ladies affiliate who raised funds for many events such as the famous Fathers' Day Pancake Breakfasts, were as active as and equal to the Mason's Eastern Star ladies.

On Easter eve in 2008, the center and St. Mary's overflowed with standees, while the next year, there were empty seats. A major change in church attendance and support had begun. The Passionist Province of St. Paul of the Cross covering the eastern United States saw the need to consolidate properties. In the preceding months, many churches and other properties had been closed. Just as the post Vatican II era of the 1960s emphasized the personal and spiritual needs of the individual, which was served by retreats, the current era needs were those of a disordered world that requires a team ministry to solve a variety of problems.

In May 2008, the decision to close was made. The center's director, Ernest Rivard, describes the closing in the Passionate newsletter for winter 2010. The closing affected many people who had considered the center a haven, but times were changing and were accepted as inevitable. Many decisions had to be made; e.g., the outdoor Stations of the Cross which included a fifteenth, the Resurrection, were moved to the Passionist Immaculate Conception Monastery at Jamaica, New York.

As in any loss, many needed to be consoled. In May 2009, the center and its now twenty-two acres were sold to Veteran's Incorporated, which provide many of the same services to troubled individuals as the Passionists had but without the religious angle.

The Passionists' facility was ideal for Vets Inc. The twenty-two-acre site has a forty thousand-square-foot building with eighty bedrooms, a multitude of classrooms, halls, a professional kitchen, and a fully functional infrastructure, as well as furniture that the priests had left.

Vets Incorporated's executive director, Denis Leary, hopes "to breathe new life into the facility but want...this amazing site to help breathe new life into our veterans." Now called *Independence Hall*, it will offer help to vets from World War II to those recently returned from Afghanistan and Iraq to "maintain their dignity, restore their spirits, and get them back on their feet."

Leary also wants the center to remain an integral part of Shrewsbury, thus the Shrewsbury Garden Club scented garden for the blind, the acreage for an organic garden, an outdoor stage at the lower end of the hill for outdoor civic events, etc.

Started in 1990 by Vietnam veterans to help their homeless, it began with the Central Massachusetts Shelter for Homeless Veterans and lease of the Massachusetts National Guard Armory for one dollar a year and many dedicated veteran volunteers of time and money. It expanded to include veterans of all wars, including women, and extended to provide "the triangle of needs" housing, employment, and health. The name was changed to *Veterans Incorporated* in 2009 as they expand into adjoining states.

How appropriate that Vets Incorporated continues as a center of hope and renewal, this time for veterans who so often have been overlooked. Chris was right. It needed to be included in the mansions as perhaps the finest of them all for its positive influence on so many lives.

MUSINGS

THE INDUSTRIAL REVOLUTION opened up a new world of growth and opportunity but an imperfect one with men being paid poorly for working ten hours a day, six days a week. Women were paid only for machine work in the shops while performing hand work at home off the clock, and children were doing dangerous work around machinery in sweatshops with only one exit, in fire traps, some into the twentieth century. While I worked in New York's garment district in the 1960s as a federal wage and hour investigator, I still found such conditions. They may well still exist in isolated areas.

The nineteenth century industrialists, such as Andrew Carnegie, were misers so obsessed in acquiring wealth that they paid starvation wages. The workers had to strike and band together as unions to be heard.

Horace Bigelow was considered strange when he gave his workers a share plan and provided affordable entertainment, even free, to the working class. What was he thinking! In the twentieth century, a small manufacturer in New England received front-page coverage when he continued to pay his employees while rebuilding his plant after a fire.

This suggests that the norm is exploitation. Let's go on into the twentieth century. The 1950s into the 1960s was a period of rebellion and unrest resulting in hippies and "angry young men" demanding change. This included "God is dead" and rejection of mores. The Beatles became a symbol of this frustration and madness spread worldwide. The *Saturday Evening Post* reprinted a story written by a top culture writer in England, "Beatles Invasion" in spring 1964 in the January–February 2014 issue. It quoted the Beatles' press officer, who said, "They're profane…and they've taken over the world. It's as if they'd founded a new religion. They're completely Antichrist."

This was the cradle of the computer conceived in the 1950s and '60s, which developed into an obsession as the computer shrank to a portable laptop that grew from personal use and a way to connect with family and friends to an open global Internet of pervasive, invasive networking at every level of use, including telephone and television. This sounds like "Big Brother is watching." I'm scared, but what do I know?

I lived it. As the lone female federal investigator in the New York office, I was sent to check ton-size computers to find who was covered by the Wage and Hour Law and who was exempt. I saw the computer shrink. I attended a university from January 1956 to September 1960, with the angry generation and the Beatle madness. The killing of President Kennedy ended "ask what you can do for the government." We became entitled and asked "what's in it for me?" Women were given "equal rights" and chose as equal the least noble male "rights." Women were given the right of choice to kill their babies—even at birth—and the human species is now depleted, which has resulted in loss of native populations and their cultures in every western nation to be replaced by multiple cultures.

Computers introduced the new era of the Internet, changing every aspect of the twenty-first century, from loss of personal privacy to individual relationships. Some are addicted and withdrawn, the Internet taking over the entire life of its members. Many reject traditional values. They seek a new reality. To do what one wants? Will we rationalize and justify?

Our World War II vets wanted to give their children everything they didn't have but failed to prepare them for the challenges of adulthood. They were "entitled" to begin where their fathers ended and could not cope. However, the inventions have been awesome and fearful. Is it time to evaluate the science and its results? Will central control help or hinder the people and their countries? Is democracy the better choice? Yes!

Restore our Constitution, freedoms of speech, religion, and media, our privacy, stability and respect for life, or the "new reality" could be central control and a nation of drones. We must restore our rights and our responsibilities for our actions.

Christians are taught to love, not judge, to "cast no stone." We did not love others as we did ourselves. Let us think "us" not "me." Let our leaders love the country, not the "party." What a refreshing and restorative change in the country that would be.

Let's join forces and try it.

We have much to gain and little to lose.

BIBLIOGRAPHY

Morrill, Hultgren, & Salomonsson "Postcard History Series-Worcester". Arcadia Pub.

Nutt, Chas. A.B. "History of Worcester and Its People" New York, 1919, Lewis Historical Pub. Co.. 4 volumns

Rice, Franklin P. "The Worcester of Eighteen Hundred and Ninety" 1919. and "Worcester of 1898".

Southwick, Albert B. "150 Years of Worcester" 1848-1998

Stone, Ora. "History of Massachusetts Industries" Vol. II, Boston: Clark Publishing. 1930

Stone, Wilbur Fiske, ed. "History of Colorado, Vol. 3, Chicago, Ill. -1918

Wood, Olive B. "Worcester-Its Past and Present" 1888

Worcester "SPY": "Married People", Glovervill, N.Y. 1845